GRANDDAUGHTER OF DUST

GRANDDAUGHTER OF DUST

POEMS

LAURA WILLIAMS

atmosphere press

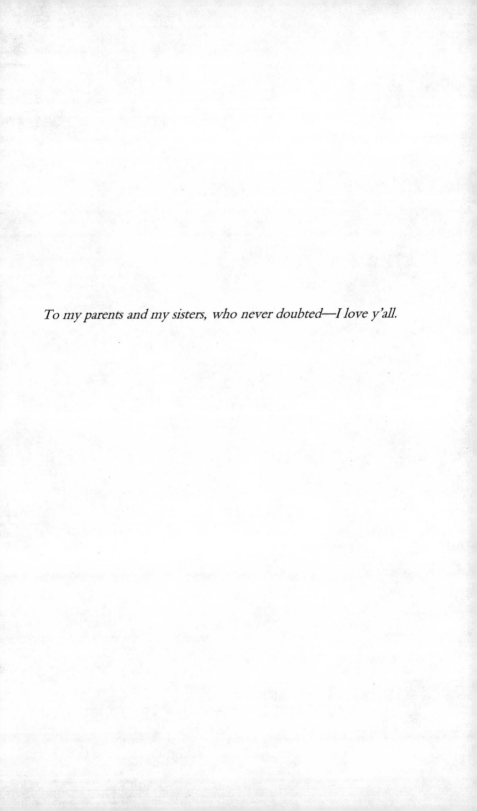

To my parents and my sisters, who never doubted—I love y'all.

TABLE OF CONTENTS

things I believed when I was five

names dripping with blood

exeunt

things i believed when i was five

"The Horse Fair"

I, breathlessly, remember when first I saw Rosa Bonheur's
The Horse Fair—so massive, vivid, precise.

   I heard the rushing hooves, the wind roaring, how the horses
   would neigh and whinny, the crack of the riding crop, the men
   shouting, thinking they had control—I've ridden horses; I'm not
   so sure those men were right.

   The stench of horse shit and sweat and dirt, tossed around
   by what should be a welcome breeze—staring at this painting, the
   size of a wall, I feel the wind move my hair, that odor slamming
   into me. It's one of the things I don't miss from my years
   with the horses.

I could reach out to touch a horse's flank—
The dapple gray, I think, because he seems
calm and the closest to me.

But my fingers touch only paint.

   The horses could prance off the wall, surely, cavort around
   me. I could tangle my fingers in a mane, another and another,
   my hands growing slick with sweat, grit in my mouth
   from the dust stirred up by a hundred horses—

But the floor is tile beneath my shoes.

   I can't leap onto a back and kick the horse into a canter,
   can't rub his nose or check his hooves for rocks,
   can't laugh as we race the wind and always lose.

I'm standing in a gallery, sterile, quiet. The horses cannot
stamp off the wall, out of pigment and into the world.

I close my eyes, going back to that girl,
awed, enamored, caught in majesty
and never released. I close my eyes,
and I see the horses. I stand there,
yearning to go back, to be the girl I was

all those years ago.

Stepping away from the wall, I open my eyes,
turn to continue on, an entire museum to explore—
But I look back. Years and a continent away,
I'm still looking back.

flutterby

flutter—
      barely a murmur
          less than a cloud
    fragile   soft
          wisp of a whisper on the wind

stained glass to steal nature's paint
          to keep what swiftly leaves

flutter—
      ever-becoming

          ever-gone

Drowning

This morning, I woke from a dream
of the ocean, that last time we went—
            you remember, don't you?
I tried to drown but
you pulled me from the waves.

I remember:
                  the hot sand beneath my feet.
                  the burning sun glaring down.
                  the salt bitter on my lips.
                  the water—
I coughed it into your mouth.

You never looked at me the same
after that. Wary. Watchful. Afraid.
You didn't understand.
I   didn't want you to understand.
I wanted to sink into the ocean,
            to let it wash me away.
I still don't know how you realized,
                  how you got to me so fast.
If I had struggled in your grasp,
            would you have
            let the ocean have me?

I remember:
                  it burned
and I
                  inhaled relief.

I dream of
                  the ocean,
                  if you hadn't been there,
                  sinking down into the deep,
                  finally at rest.

My family thanked you, when
I was still strapped to

the bed.
    I never did.

      You   remember, don't you?
I'll never   forget.

Heritage (Theft)

they fall

                                    one
                    by
                        one

roll out of the nest
                        and smash on the ground

Baby flutters growing wings
                    coos softly
                        nestles in
                            gobbles and gorges and gulps

Baby grows on the broken eggshell of never-siblings

                        Mama knows she didn't lay that egg
                            but this is the only Baby left

Progression

Define *civilized.*

> Civilization—society,
> Culture groups.

What is being civilized?
Who decides, and why?
It matters by choice, by decision,
By concentrated effort and violent force.

Define *civilization.*

> Its purpose, its aim;
> A creation of who, for who;
> When, where, why—

Basic questions.
The basic questions,
With no answer despite millennia of thought.

Tell me what *civilized* is:

> Its purpose, its aim,
> Its reason of invention;
> What it was created for,
> Who it was created by.

Ask: why do you ask?

> Are you civilized enough to wonder?

Civilization is needed for thought—

> Thought civilizes.
> > Be civilized,
> > > have thought.

You are nothing before civilization,
A beast—

> A beast? Define *beast.*

Tell me:

> Who are you to *civilize* me?

Define *civilized.*

Lessons

i'll be your monster
        baby
just like you created me to be
and when i'm tearing it all down
don't blame me
remember this is what you wanted
i'm just doing as you say

i won't be sorry

i tried to run away
to walk and to fly
i tried to swim away
instead i drowned
and the water carried me back
i washed up on the shore
legs and wings long torn
i washed up on the shore
just in time for sunrise
and you gathered me up
pieced me back together

you broke me instead
glued me all wrong

i'll be your monster
        baby
it's all i know how to be

you break me
      are breaking me
      will be breaking me
      have broken me
      broke me

every moment i breathe
i breathe because you let me
i think i once knew that was wrong
you've broken me so many times

i can't remember how it felt to be whole

shattered
tattered
scattered
spread across the bed
discarded on the floor
you take and take and take
i know it wasn't always this way

you can be so gentle

you don't like it when i shout
                    when i pull away
you don't mind my tears though
                    my bruises
you wipe away the blood
                    so gently

you piece me back together
when you're finished breaking me

you kiss me when i'm frightened
you ignore me when i'm angry

i'm your monster
            baby
don't you like what you've made?

i'm your monster
            baby
don't you want to me break you?

it's not like i know anything else
it's not like you're owed anything less

i'll light the fire
            baby
burn everything down
i'll light the fire
            baby

this is my moment of reclamation
because i was someone before your touch
and i'm gonna be that someone again

i don't want to be your monster
      baby

this is what you made
but i'll make myself anew
and that'll be the last lesson i learn from you

SeaShore

          Salt on the air,
taste   on my lips.
          Grains   in my hair,
rough pinpricks
          against my skin.

Stand on the beach,
warm sand
          against my feet:
Look into never-ending forever,
          feel so small,
insignificant.

Wonder:
          Against this vastness,
how can I matter?

Eyes closed,
          feet subsumed
          with ancient water,
          horizon stretching
          infinitely in front
          and manufactured cathedrals to
                    impermanence in back —

I matter because
          I am not eternal.
I matter because,
          unlike the ocean,
                    I remember.

Run

Get in the car, turn the key,
        (make sure to buckle up 'cause,
        trust me, flying out the windshield
        ain't a good ending)
blast the music, put the windows down,
        and go.

A mile turns to two turns to three:
        your shoulders loosen,
        you can breathe.
Three turns to four turns to five:
        stuck at a redlight,
        but the interstate's up on the left.
Six takes you through the light, down the ramp.
        (gotta merge: why can't everyone
        be as good a driver as you?)
Windows go up, music louder,
dark clouds rolling behind you—
but there's pavement in front,
        and you go.

Seven eight nine ten—
        a blur.
Scream along with the music,
no tears in your eyes,
no regret streaming behind you.
You go.

Eleven twelve thirteen.
        Speed limits are guidelines.
        If you drive fast enough far enough,
            you'll escape.
Forget it all.
Nothing behind you.
Nothing chasing.
Nothing waiting.

You go.
You drive.

Fast enough.
Far enough.

Dark clouds behind you;
clear sky ahead.
Buckled tight, music blasting.
Gotta fill up sometime; gotta sleep.
But 'til then—

You just go.

Oh, I Wish

the world was smaller then—
or maybe that was just me.
I could do anything,
fly and swim and run.
I could be anything,
a pirate, a princess, a hired gun.
Mama was so smart,
she could solve anything;
Daddy was so strong and warm.

I miss the naps in kindergarten.
I miss my problems being solved by someone else.

the world is small now—
or maybe that's just me.
I'm so much taller,
not smarter but wiser maybe.
there's so much to do,
so much to see.

I'll always miss the naps in kindergarten,
and so many problems still get to me.
if I could go back—
well, who's to say?

soot-stained

It aches
continually:
>My body.
>My heart.
>My soul.
So tired,
I trudge on.

I wish it were over
but time alone heals,
>so they say.
This too shall pass,
>so they say.
Trudging,
I hold on.

Dreaming,
asleep or awake?
Yes—
always yes.
Minutes, days, weeks,
months are gone
but it feels like just yesterday—

Time heals.
Hurt fades.
Memory softens.
Soon again my soul will sing—
>everyone says.

Hope is all I have now,
hope that they are right
and this too will pass.
This will pass.
Asleep or awake, it all feels the same,
but it will pass.

I trudge.
I crawl.

I weep.
—I hope

—I hope—

Trudging,
I hold on.
—Hoping,
        I hold on.

Personal Growth

Here you are, back again in the bar you know
I visit every evening when work has left me angry
and sad. Here you are, smiling and laughing like you
never walked away with me crying in the street. Here
you are, toasting the whole room, making friends who don't
know what a terrible person you are inside beneath the
grinning eyes and brilliant smile. Here you are, back again
as if you'd never left.

                        Fine, sit down, share a
drink with me—But I won't take you home this
time. It's *my* home now; I painted you out of
the walls. You're not welcome so don't come 'round. We'll
talk here or not at all. Keep your hands on
your side of the table because your touch is something
I don't crave anymore.

                        Oh, you're sorry now? The sentiment's
too little and years too late. I'm glad you've got
your act together, but what's that got to do with
me? I burnt all your pictures ages ago. I'm not
even angry anymore, just a bit relieved. See, *darling*, I
didn't know it then but I'm so much better off
without you. My life's on track and I'm happy. So
here's a toast to you, glad you're doing well, but
that's *all* the time I'll waste on you.

                        Don't pout
at me; I've grown past it. No, I don't care
if you cry. You didn't care when you walked away
and I won't spend another moment of my time helping
you find yourself. I'm done here tonight. Thank you for
this chance to see that I have everything I wanted
and you're not part of that at all. Oh, don't
cry, sweetheart; it didn't work for me, either. I wish
you luck but that's the last thought I'll grant you.

Lay Down (and sleep)

lay down your head and sleep
they preach
rest because
the work is done
rest because
your sorrows are through
rest because
peace awaits
with no more tomorrows ahead

lay down your head and sleep
they promise

what they don't tell you
there is
no peace
no silence
no rest
what they don't tell you
is that once you're laid down
all you have is endless tomorrows
and knowing that you'll
never
have another chance

what they don't tell you
regrets are forever

lay down your head and sleep
they preach
not knowing   in the way of the living

that it is a sorrowful lie

the living say
lay down your head and sleep
the dead cry
oh don't wish your life away

Skin Shed

i have lived
lifetimes
without you—

(oh, my once-love)

it was good.

these fingertips have never
        touched
you.
these lips and this tongue have never
        tasted
you.
these eyes have never
        seen you
nor have
these ears
        heard you.

this lifetime,
and the last,
and the one before,
and all the rest,

i haven't caught your
scent
once.

it has been good,
my once-love,

these lives without you—

and yet here you are,
begging for one more chance.

i have lived lifetimes
without you.

i've grown, learned,
become.

you are a
once, a
no longer, a
never again.

hear me this final time.

i gave you one life.
all the lives since
have been better,

these lifetimes without you—

you want another chance.
i tell you,

no.

i have

become.

in all these lifetimes,
you haven't learned.

i have lived
lifetimes
without you;
i shall continue
to live
lifetimes
without you.

and, my
never-again-love,

they shall be good.

Oceanic

i forget the taste of the sea
until i cry
and the tears drip over my lips,
and as i gasp for air,
i taste my tears
and there it is—
the ocean in my mouth.

i'm sorry.
i left you in the waves.
wind whipping my hair,
i watched you drown.
i forgot—

they say the deep waters are dark;
monsters lurk past the horizon.
ships are lost out in the deep,
and i dream that you're there waiting for me.

i forgot the taste of the ocean.
i stand in the storm.
i long to taste your tears,
to wrap around you like when we were young—
        we were so young
        the first time we stepped onto the beach,
        let the waves lap at our feet.
        we were so hungry then,
        waiting for the sea to swallow us whole.

i cry and i cry,
your name on my tongue,
the way you laughed,
how we danced—
our hearts beat in time;
our souls sang together.
we stood in the sun and the storm,
promised, swore, made solemn vows.
i memorized your freckles once—
i've forgotten so much now.

i miss you.
i don't go to the shore anymore.
i only taste the sea when i weep.
i remember you then,
your laughter on the wind—
you loved the ocean so

                                     i left you in the waves.

Questions Never Asked

I remember the questions I never asked
        because I knew they wouldn't be answered,
        because I knew that to ask
            would show what I was thinking
            and that what I was thinking was wrong.
I remember never seeing who I thought I was
        in the lessons, whatever the lesson was.
I remember how my mind wandered
        because it couldn't be contained
            by those hypocritical walls,
        by my peers who were never on the same page,
            not even in the same book.
I remember thinking, sometimes,
        that something was wrong with me
but if I ever verbalized it outside my head,
I don't remember who to or when.

Looking back with my adult self's eyes,
with years of knowing who I am,
        I understand.
Knowing parts of my story that I didn't then,
family secrets, the diagnosis I was never told,
and how many more kinds of humans there are
than that school will ever admit,
        I understand.

I want to tell that girl I was—
        It's alright, you're not wrong.
        You're not incomplete. You're not broken.
        It's not your fault you don't understand.
        It's not a problem to be fixed.
I want to tell that girl I was—
        Even when you're almost thirty,
        you're still looking for who you are
        but you'll get there, baby girl,
        you'll get there.
I want to tell her—
        You're not broken for what you can't do.
        You're not broken for what you don't feel.

And—

You're not broken for what you don't understand.
Baby girl, you're not broken in the least.

Not All

This war will never be over
while anyone walks afraid, alone or in a crowd,
scared that
   someone somewhere
will be that one.
   Not all,
you say.
   Not all
   are like that.
   Not all
   are that way.
You know what that means?
You know what I hear?
You say,
   Not all
and I hear,
   Someone somewhere.

One is too many,
and I walk afraid,
   heart in my throat,
   scream in my mouth,
   eyes constantly searching
   for the threat I know exists—
     Someone somewhere.
   Not all?
Too many.

This war between us will never be
over
while you
refuse
to hear what I mean,
while you
preach that
   Not all
 are that way.

There shouldn't be a war.
> *Not all?*
> *Someone somewhere*
who takes and takes and takes.
I may be someone's mother,
someone's sister, daughter, aunt, niece.
Someone somewhere loves me and maybe they're like you—
But I'm myself and my own.
I breathe and I cry and I write and I sing;
I live and I love and I hate.
I'm my own before I'm anyone's
and that's enough.
There shouldn't be a war
but I'll fight.
> *Not all*, no—
But I'll fight that
> *someone somewhere.*

I walk afraid in the dark and that's stupid,
in this world with
> *someone somewhere*
waiting to strike,
that
> *someone somewhere*
who takes and takes.

You say,
> *Not all*
like that fixes things,
like it should matter that
nine out of ten aren't monsters.
One is too many,
and excuses are useless
with blood on the ground,
and hearts in throats,
and tears and tears.

> This is my body;
> I'll not break it for you.

Don't say,

Not all.
Don't ignore that anyone walks afraid.
Don't tell me things are my fault
and then stare down my shirt,
or follow me telling me to smile.
Don't laugh when I say I'm nervous
because that man is still out there and I
don't want him to know which car is mine.
Don't say,
        Not all
and expect a pat on the back
because this is
my
world too and that's
not good enough.
It never has been.
I won't accept it anymore.

Don't say,
        Life's not fair.
I know that.
Don't say,
        Not all
when you just mean,
        Not me
when you're really saying,
        I'd never do that
when the words you want are,
        Not my problem.
It's everyone's problem,
and I won't be quiet.
I won't turn away.
I'll walk afraid in the dark
knowing that
        someone somewhere
will take and take.

Don't say,
        Not all
because that just means
        Some.

You think that fixes things?
You think that's acceptable?
Don't tell me that
          someone somewhere
is a monster
and I should be
grateful
because it's
not   you.

This is a   war
and I'll fight and fight
because I am
my own
and I should have
that unalienable right
to walk alone and unafraid
anywhere and anytime.

You say
          Not all,
and I say
          Too many.

And I say,
          Enough.

things I believed when I was five

Daddy's as tall as a tree
Mama's always right
I'll always be bigger
      than my baby sister
my big sister will always
      be able to help me
my brother's the best
the dog lives forever
and one day
      one day
           I'll know what to do no matter what
              one day when I'm grown up like you

Night

We have forgotten how it felt when
warmth fell down from the sky.
Ages ago, a light burned bright

high up there in the sky,
little lights dotting the night.
How warm it must've been,

how bright and beautiful.
Legends tell of that star above
and legends tell of how it died.

Look: do you see the light of the fire
thrown up and out into the sky? It
lit everything aglow; so beautiful, it must've been.

We have forgotten and only have
stories now. It is so cold.
Listen: do you know what *daylight* means?

Once the sky was warm. Once, stars
could be seen. Fire fades, it seems,
embers and ashes and a long ago dream.

Once, a fire lit the sky and all
was alive, and I remember the
stories my grandmother would tell—

Come, my love, sit by the fire.
It is the very last of all
and when it goes—

Listen and do not fear; let my words
warm you, cling tight to my hand.
Once, all was warm and bright,

until the warmth fell from the sky.
But before that, oh, it was so grand—
It is dark now, always. But once,

I swear to you, there were
lights that lit up the night.
Look.

Mo(u)rning

Where does grief go
when it finally fades and floats away?
Is it   relief, the lightening of a load;
is it   hope, rushing into your soul,
                    lifting you up, letting you think,
                    if only for a single moment
                    and not a breath more,
            that happiness might sink back into your bones,
                    barren for so long, cold and weary?

Grief consumes, ravenous and slavering,
until all you feel is exhaustion,
broken and weak,   like nothing
will ever ease the pain, the emptiness.
But when it finally splinters,
            what is left?
Hope? Relief? Anything? No—
                              —thing.

When the grief floats away,
where does it go?
            Does it settle somewhere else,
            take root, spread pain and fear and anger
                    —despair—
            where before there existed something?

Grief subsumes, washing away
everything anything nothing something—

                                    All.

Where does grief go when it fades
and what is left   when it goes?
Relief? The resurrection of hope?
A trench so deep it'd never be possible to climb free?
Can relief sweep you up,
                    fly you out,
                              cocoon around you,
                                    let you sleep?
Can hope warm what is frozen,
                    bloom what is barren?

What happens? What remains?
When hurts heal—slowly,
                    softly—
            When hurts heal—
                        Hurts heal—

When grief finally fades and floats away,
where does it go?
What is left in its absence?
        Perhaps relief settles in, spreading
                    fragile wings, shifting
                    fragile muscles, stretching
                    towards a light, far in the distance,
                    a light shining softly, hesitantly,
                                hopeful—

            Hope, the strength, the
                    thought that surviving leads
                        eventually to something else—

Grief devours, digests, spits out
        someone you don't know but
        who seems familiar, similar,
        an echo, a distorted reflection,
        a *was* become an *is*.
When grief goes, a new person is left, someone
                with fresh scars,
                with divots,
                with sore spots that will
                    (perhaps)
                always be tender.
Hurt heals, when grief is survived.

Grief goes. Where? Away.
You   remain.
You breathe, you cry, you smile—
        You live.

Grief fades and floats away.
You remain.

You live.

I Could Lie

i could tell you a thousand pretty things—

i could smile and laugh
and it might wipe away the pain

i could pretend just like you
i could lie here and now
just for the chance you won't
walk away when the words fade into the wind

but all that leaves us with
is this same moment
because i know it'll come around again

i could lie
but the truth is that   i'm tired

i could lie
but the truth is that   the bed's cold even when you're here

i could lie
but the truth is that   i'm not sure a few days' respite is worth it

i could lie
i could spin you a dream
of what we haven't been in so long
i could smile and laugh
but i'm almost sure you'd see through it

i could lie
but instead i'll just ask once more

are you sure this is what you want?

The Dark Birds Caw

This isn't how I wanted the story to end:
    murders
    and funerals
    and the dark birds' caw.

Roses grow on the grave,
        red as blood.
Written on the stone is a name.
Birds caw
    and shriek
    and scream.
In the dirt, I gave it all away.

I remember that night—
    You smirked at me,
        eyes grinning,
    and I felt so in love.

For a moment, so brief, so bright,
I was sure we'd be happy,
you and me together,
    hand in hand,
    heart to heart,
    dancing and laughing,
and oh, we planned so much.

You told me a beautiful fairy tale
but I told you the same,
and on the grave there is a name.

Murders and funerals, dark birds in the sky.
Of course it's raining;
    it was the night we met.

I had hopes, dreams, expectations,
the world at my feet
and a brilliant future ahead.
I was so young then.
Now, now, the dark birds career.

And the name, the name,
I trace the words and my fingers bleed;
thorns bite deep.
And the name, the name—
Murders and funerals, and a midnight sky so deep—

It rained the night I died,
  tumbling into your arms when my feet slipped
  lowering you into the ground,
  trudging away while dark birds shrieked overhead.

This isn't how I wanted the story to end,
murders and funerals.
It began blindingly brilliant
in a lovely fairy tale lie
but here we are—

Murders and funerals,
and in the dark sky,
dark birds cry.

Lighting up the Kerosene

This is me, lighting up the kerosene,
listening to the ghosts scream,
        and I won't stop.

Don't tell me how it's not
worth it, I should be quiet
now, not when you're in the
ground. Haunt me please—I'm begging.
Should I get on my hands
and knees? I'll scream it out.

You shouldn't have left if you
didn't want me to lose it
all. You should've stayed forever, like
we swore, standing on that burning
shore. We promised; we promised it
all out loud. And I'll light
it all now—I mean it,
        I'll burn it all down.

I want to hear you; can't
you hear me now? I want
to hear you—scream it for
me now. Don't tell me to
be quiet, not when you're in
the ground. Don't tell me it's
not worth it, not when it's
all I have left, not when
you broke our promise. Haunt me,
        please.

I'm lighting up the kerosene.
Please let me hear the ghosts scream.
Please let me hear you say my name—
        Can't you hear me screaming yours?

Survivor

In the mirror, I see your face.
      I look like you
&
      it haunts me every day.
I have your   eyes,
the way your   lips twist.
I have your   nose
&
I still remember how you
      kiss.

I wish I could forget all those years

but I know I never
      will.
It made me
      who I am
&
      how I survive
It gave me
      strength,
      living with all your lies.
It proved to me
      I could escape

 & I see your face—

But now I have the
power to look away.

I close my eyes
& I shut that door
I look like you
but I am not yours.

Not anymore.

I see your face every day
      & I know I got away;

& I smile with lips
just like yours;
& my eyes,
        well, they're not,
        not anymore.

None of me is yours.

I got   away.
I learned to   survive.
        & you may haunt me,
        & I may cry
        'cause I remember but
        because of you I now thrive.

I learned so much;
I became strong;
& in the mirror I see your face
& I know I can move on.

I see your face in the mirror
& I turn away.
I close the door.
I am not yours.

None of me is yours anymore.

Resurrected Trees

There are resurrected trees on my desk
at work
taking up space usually left
for my refillable water bottle
and the hours I alone keep:
        nearly half a dozen of Freire,
        a collection of essays on social studies,
        adult literacy studies—
I've skimmed most of them,
read some a bit deeper,
and now they're waiting on me to
write a paper so amazing the
ink on the cyber page sings.
        I have hundreds of books.
I'm reading one now that
talks about odes to the ordinary
so I chose that stack of books.
        Because   I wrote a poem
                        a few days ago that
                        hurts to reread.
        Because   I'm sinking down
                        and need a hand up.
        Because   I'm frightened and lonely.
        Because   I'm so tired I can't sleep.
        Because   reading is my passion.
        Because   writing is my passion.
When I don't know what to do,
I just start typing
or I pick up a pen
and I discover what words want to spill out.

        So this is my ode to the ordinary,
        my attempt at finding joy
        in the everyday,
        my try at keeping the grief at bay.

I have papers to write,
books to read,
classes to attend,

a job to do when my boss gives me work.
But I'll keep reading.
I'll keep picking up the pen.

And when it all starts to weigh me down,
I'll remember
how it feels
finding the word that fits in perfectly,
knowing that I am right when I declare,

"I am born a poet."

The Last Poem

The last poem died yesterday.
I buried it beneath the oak—
you know the one, you planted it ages
ago when poetry was young.

The poem, the very last of all—it told me
your secrets. It whispered about the
ocean's depths and the height of the sky.
I listened in wonder; I'd never heard
such words before. The poem sounded like you,
my dear, how you sang before you left here.

You never sang for me.
I listened through the wall,
catching what words I could.
I still have some, hidden behind the wallpaper.
I kept them, just in case.
You never came back for them, though,
just like you never came back for me.

The oak tree is dying.
Soon enough, I'll have to cut it down
or it might fall on the house.
What will happen then
to the bones of the last poem?

With the tree gone,
how will I remember your song?
Everything here grows old.
If I can't remember your song,
will you have ever sung at all?

The last poem died yesterday.
I buried it with all the rest,
the memories you left behind when you left.
I dream, sometimes, that the bones sprout,
that from sorrow hope grows.
That perhaps, somewhere in the world,
more songs and poems are born.

But I buried the last poem just yesterday,
beneath a dying oak.

Revolution

The sun burns
if you let
it shine on

you too long.
How long is
too long? Learn

by being burned.
The sun gives
life by shining.

You remember the
burn from the
scars, from the

transformation of being
set aflame and
after somehow surviving.

Where I'm From

Go outside and it slams into me:
The air thick and humid,
So heavy it weighs me down.
I know where I am even before a single step.

The wind carries the scent on the breeze
Once the rain is past.
The world smells new, warm,
Like the dirt I played in when I was young.

A jumble of ingredients—
I once told Mama that Daddy was doing it wrong.
A spoonful of butter and sugar,
Chocolate chips that melted in my hand, on my tongue.

We sit around the table long into the night,
Cups refilled endlessly, nibbling on fruit and crackers,
Telling well-worn stories and ancient in-jokes—
They aren't funny but we laugh every time.

names dripping with blood

Toil

I clean the kitchen:

Wash and dry the dishes. Clear and wipe
the counters. Soap the tiles, scrubbing until my
skin cracks, my knees ache, my shoulders. Breathe
through the tears. I breathe, kneeling on the
floor. It hurts as I stand. I stand
and I breathe. Sweep once everything is done.

For now, the kitchen sparkles.
I'll clean it again tomorrow.

Names Dripping with Blood

Once, there was a princess
beloved
by all who knew her.

Her name?
> We do not speak it now.
But I can tell you
> of the court she commanded,
>> of the besotted knights
>> and the charming princes
> battling for the honor
>> of kissing her hand,
>>> for scraps of her attention,
>>>> for a kiss and a dance.
I can tell you
> of the far-flung kingdoms
> and the nobles of the land
> who offered fortunes and favors
> simply for the chance
> of marrying the most beautiful princess
> the world had ever seen.

Was she?
> Debatable,
> but not where anyone can hear.

Once, there was a princess.
No, she was not cursed.

She wed on a bright spring day
to the second son of the king's greatest ally.
Their union was a blessing for both kingdoms—

or so it seemed, at first.

His name?
> Long forgotten.
> It was never important, nor he.

The beloved princess's father
     died
the autumn after the wedding.
She was crowned queen in mourning black.
Her husband
     died
the following spring,
while she grew plump with his child.

Oh, how the kingdom mourned them both!
     None cried so beautifully as the beloved queen.

She birthed a son in the summer.
     His name…
Well, it is one you know.

Tell me, have you heard of the witch
who lives far beyond the mountains,
past that haunted forest,
down near the frozen shore?
     Yes?
And have you heard of the warlord
whose reach stretches from ocean to ocean,
who gobbles up realms and spits out the bones?

Of course you have.

The beloved princess who
became the beloved queen
was not cursed, no.

     She *was* the curse, you see.

Who cast it?
No one knows.
Why?

Lips as red as the blood shed
     when a prince was sacrificed
          by the light of the moon.

Hair as black as the moonless night
      a queen recited words in a language
          long lost to time.
Skin as white as the bones that
      litter battlefields across
          a continent.

We are cursed, you see.

Her name?
      We do not say it,
      though once it rang out in cheers,
      echoing off the stone streets.
His name?
      There are some who whisper it.
      You would know it if you heard.

Mine?
Oh, that is unimportant, I promise you.
You shouldn't wonder such things, you know.
It matters not how I remember.
Best get on home, now.
Don't stray from the path.

We are cursed, you see.
Our beloved princess became
the terrible witch
who rules the world from the seashore.
Her beloved son became
the horrible warlord
who commands the world from a throne of bones.

It was centuries ago, now.
Don't ask me how I remember.
I promise, you don't want to know.

Dew Drops

She watches the dew drip from the rose, clear
drop after clear drop, counting her breaths slowly,
carefully, drop by drop, breath by breath. The sun
glints off the dew. She reaches, hoping to feel some of
the warmth—But the light is beyond her grasp. Her
arm falls as she lowers her head, counting her breath,
watching the glint. Somewhere in the halls, someone
screams, someone begs, someone dies. Her turn will come
soon, she knows. So she focuses on the dew, on the sun,
 makes a story of a rescue, of love and a kiss.

But no one will come.
No one has come, as
she's grown old. Sunlight glints
on the dew
on the rose
and she breathes,
waiting,
             counting
                      each
                              breath.

Danced All Night (Silver Shadow)

Glittering gown, sparkling slippers,
music spirals, dancers twirl—
Such a night, so bright,
never to come again.

> *The prince! The prince*
> *will choose a bride!*

Splendid, glistening—
jewels,   eyes

> —hunger
> desire—

The prince chases a silver shadow.
> gown and slippers
> made of glass
> carved from air
Music trails after, laughter, shock—
Courtiers murmur long into the night.

Glass shatters on stone.

> *The prince!*
> *The prince!*
> *Seeks a silver shadow*
> *for his bride!*

> (mad? some ask
> oh, yes, some answer)

The prince yearns,
pines, fades
into a shadow.

Glittering gown, sparkling slippers.
People remember her,
the silver shadow.
Her eyes gleam as bright

as the crown on her hair,
jeweled rings, luminous bracelets,
opulent chains adorning her neck.

The prince!
The prince's health!
Pray for him to heal!

She shimmers,
she who will be queen.
The silver shadow gleams
on the throne
as the prince lingers in a languishing sleep.

(she is such a faithful, dutiful wife! some say)

(none dare disagree)

Wolf

She wears a cloak of fury and fire, hiding her
drab moth-wings and porcelain skin. The hood is always up,

shielding her ebon-straw hair from the harsh elements that fade
it further away from the raven's-wing it used to be.

Mama doesn't know, doesn't want to know, and eyes can't
see what the mind won't acknowledge. So Mama just sews

and sews, blind to the fallen child across the dinner
table. And Papa, she's still his little girl but she

stopped being little long ago. The forest is cold as
she trudges through it, feet shuffling in the snow, clutching

her threadbare cloak, frayed, torn and unraveling and not warm
at all, closer about her shoulders. The ruby bled from

it years ago. Her footprints fade into the snow. Threads
of a crimson cloak flutter in the icy breeze, threads

with no cape to be seen. Here a faded hair,
there a faded hair, and look! There a bloodstain. She

wore that cloak to shield herself from the world and
its pain—Mama sewed that cape and Mama carried her

to term and Mama now weeps in Papa's arms, because
the Wolf, as always, has won. She was Papa's little

girl. But she stopped being little long ago and her
cloak of fury and fire could not mask the scars.

She was Papa's little girl—
       and what's his stays his.

The Wolf licked
his lips and
his fangs glistened
in the moonlight.
The Wolf laughed
and dug a
hole for her
fragile little bones.

Thorn's Bite

the thorns bite deep,
tearing skin to the bone.
skulls grin from the ground;
pale fingers cling to the vines.
swords, rusted dull,
languish in the dirt.

one after another after another,
year after year after year,
they bravely quest to the
cursed castle to kiss
the princess and claim the crown.

the curse devours them,
their blood and soul feeding
the magic, strengthening it
year after year after year.

the thorns bite deep,
pull him down.
the next arrives, stepping
over the rusting sword.
ignoring the grimacing skull,
the pale ribs crumbling to dust.

the thorns bite deep.

Apples

Poison drips down her throat.

The apple is crisp, juicy,
a tiny bit sour,
firm in her hand,
such a brilliant red.

Too late, she recognizes those
cold, cold eyes.
She collapses, cruel laughter
loud in her ears.
The apple still smells delicious
as it rolls from her fingers.

She dreams—
dark locks and crimson drops
on virgin snow
a wish granted
a life taken for the cost

She dreams—
Silent
Stagnant
—trapped in glass,
no dancing, no music,
no joy
pinned butterfly in stepmother's web

She wakes, jolted from dreaming,
falls onto dirt and roots.
She breathes deeply;
the cool air soothes her still-burning throat.

"My love!" she hears and looks up.
His eyes are colder than his voice is warm.
She gazes at him, his handsome face, his luxurious clothes
and feels poison
drip
down

                                    her
                                        throat.

A deep breath fills her lungs.
She gathers her feet beneath her,
glancing at the men around what
must be a prince, surrounding her, and again
he proclaims, "My love!"

                    Love, she thinks. *Love?*
                            —Am I dreaming still?

She rises, noticing that the
dress swirling around her ankles
is not the
ragged gown
she wore when she
bit into the apple.

                    (How long has she slept?)

The prince holds out a hand,
smooth and pale, fingers long and slim.

She fled one cage,
            was caught in another,
                        and will not be trapped in a third.

She smells apples on the air.
Cold eyes pin her in place;
the prince's men murmur, stepping closer.
The prince bares his teeth in a sharp smile.

She takes a deep breath,
                            releases it slow.
            "I thank you, my lord,"
she says gracefully,
                    softly,
            "for waking me."

And she runs.

She knows not how long she slept
but these trees she knows.

The men follow, shouting—

She darts into the woods,
        freed by poison,
                the only kind thing her father's wife has ever
done.

She dreams of poison   d
                                r
                                    i
                                        p
                                        p
                                            i
                                            n
                                        g

                            d
                            o
                        w
                    n
            her throat
                    and wakes

                                    ravenous.

Shorn

She shaves her head,
after.

Carefully, with a
newly-forged blade,
the king's barber's steady hands
reveal her skull's pale skin.

"You'll set a new fashion trend, Highness," the barber tells her.

She smiles into the mirror,
trailing her fingertips along the
crown of her head.

"I thank you, sir," she says as
the barber bows his way
from the room.

She never does let
her hair
grow
long again.

Tower

they told me
i was the fairest
when they locked me away in the tower.

it was a gift,

given by a fairy
when i was only three.

they told me
it was to protect me,
only to keep me safe,
that one day i would be free,

when
love's chosen
came for me.

but how can
love's chosen

know me

when i barely

know myself?

he'll be handsome,
they told me;
he'll be brave and strong and true.
he'll be a warrior able to beat the greatest foe—

but will he be patient?
will he be kind?

will he help me discover
everything
i was forced to leave behind?

magically,
every morn and every eve,
a sumptuous meal appeared for me
and so i never hungered.
but each time it was roast duck—

do you know how many times
you can eat the same thing
before it becomes
ash
in your mouth?

magically,
every eve,
there appeared
a tub of warm water, soap, and a cloth.

every morn and every eve,
i studied the magic.
every morn and every eve,
for more years than i can tell.

finally i wove a rope
from the bedclothes,
from my dresses,
from even my hair,
and i strengthened it
with a spell of my own.

and i climbed
down
the side
of that tower.

if
love's chosen

wants me,

he can come

find me

and we'll see then

what love
thinks
is
worthy.

Gingerbread

Hunger hunger
Hungry eyes
Here they come
Feast all night
Fatten up the juicy entrée
Enslave the petite morsel on the plate
Hunger hunger
Almost time
Clever girl

Swan Brother

Oh, how I remember before—
we chased each other, laughed,
played where we liked while
the nurse shouted for us
to be calm, steady, princes.
We knew our place, then.

I remember—cracking,
tearing, screaming. Suddenly
I was shorter,
I had no
hands, I stared
up and up,
        and my father's wife smiled down,
        lips red as the blood my
        dying mother coughed onto satin sheets,
        and she said,
            Fly, little princes,
            or for dinner
            I'll roast swan.

Our sister's cries followed us into the sky.

We learned to speak to
each other. We used our
bills to write with sticks.
We discovered what we could
eat, relearned to drink, avoided
hunters, both human and animal,
and we lived. We lived,
no longer princes. We flew.

She found us, our sweet
little sister. She found us
but did not speak. I
brought her a stick and
she scratched out her painful,
lengthy quest. We circled her
and offered what comfort we

could. We guarded her as
she worked. We learned to
speak with her, and treasured
each silent laugh, each smile.
She grew from girl to
woman, scarring her hands, toughening
her skin, never eating, never
sleeping enough. I wanted to
tell her that we weren't
worth it, us brash no-longer-princes.
We had done nothing to
earn such a stalwart sister.
And she harvested, and she
sewed, and so seasons passed.

We were almost too late.
We dove from the sky,
shrieking a warning, the soldiers
scattering beneath us. Despite the
rope around her, our little
sister threw the shirts into
the air and we lunged
into them, one by one.

Through her relieved laughter, my
sister wept. I told her,
> It'll be fine,
> little one, dearest.
> It'll be fine.

Before—the years are hazy when
I was young, when I was
a swan. My older brothers have
returned to our home or gone
out into the world, seeking adventure—
of which I have had enough
to last a lifetime. My wing
is a reminder I can never
escape. I live here in my
sister's court, telling tales to amuse
courtiers, to amuse children, to amuse

servants as they work, to make
my sister laugh, when I can.

I remember before—
I miss being a
swan
far more than I miss being a
prince.

Freedom's Flight

I tell you the story of a horse born of blood
who danced across the sky. Gods and men alike
hungered to ride the wingéd steed daring to fly.
But such a beast, created from death, could
surely only be cursed. He neighed a warning,
bugled from one end of the earth to the other

for none could catch, much less tame, a son of
the horizon. And how they tried, men and gods
alike, foolish and lusting, with bridle and tack
formed for no less a purpose than harnessing a
moonbeam; they chased after the horse
born of blood, seeking to tame a star.

I tell you now, as my mother told me, twirling
in her fingers a feather of stardust and water.
There are some things, daughter, she said,
feather dancing across her fingers, *that cannot
be broken. There are some things,* she
murmured, gazing up at a dark sky full of stars,

*that gods and men alike will break themselves
trying to break.* Holding out a feather pale as
bone, long as my forearm, she laughed, *There
are some things, child, that men and gods alike
will never understand.* I tell you now,
as my mother told me, for you are my daughter

and old enough now to know. There is a horse
born of blood who dances across the sky.
He returns when he wishes to, for treats and
somewhere to rest. He does not come when
called—Remember that. He is not tamed,
has never been broken. But as he was born

of blood, and as we bleed with the cycle of the moon,
daughter, he is ours as we are his. Remember,
my sweet—Men and gods alike long to ride him
far up in the sky, horizon to horizon. What they

seek to take, he offers to us freely. Magic
does as it wills, whatever gods or men say.

Look to the sky.
Freedom is
ours,
as long as we know it
cannot be
tamed.

Selkie Queen

Once   (so the story goes)
a prince wandered along a forgotten shore,
seeking shells and precious stones.
He was a collector, you see,
and what he found he'd not gone looking for.
Does this pardon him for what came next?
Well   (even now)   that's fiercely debated
among scholars and historians.
But that is not important for this tale.
For this tale, we need only know
that he found what none had seen before.
Does it excuse him?
We won't bother with that.

This prince, handsome and charming,
beloved the realm over for his candor and his grace—
if he'd known, some of us ask,
would he have done the same?
No matter.   What's done is done.
And he, our graceful prince,
as he walked along the shore
            without his courtiers,
            without his guards,
he found a luxurious fur whose like he'd never felt before.
And so our young prince,
he examined it and then, our sad prince,
he brought it home.
Without telling a soul,
                        he brought it home.

Not long after he hid the skin in his elegant rooms
            (how did a servant not find it?
            did they and not tell?
            had they but told—
            but as far as is known,
            no one knew),
a woman came to court.
Dark of hair and dark of eyes,

dressed in finery not seen in years,
well-spoken and straight-spined,
she asked for an audience with the prince.
It was granted, of course.
He was   gracious, our prince.

The woman spoke of a lost treasure,
                            stolen
while   innocently
she bathed, and demurely demanded of the prince
what he would do with such a brazen, disrespectful thief.
Our prince spoke valiantly
of   honor
and   nobility,
and the woman smiled, lips red as blood.
She thanked the prince for his time,
curtsied gracefully, and turned to leave—
oh, if only the prince had not risen from his throne!
If only the prince, that sunny day, had let the woman go.

But true the tale must be told.

The prince asked her to dine with him,
            asked her for her story,
            asked her for her name.
And the more she spoke,
the more he fell in love.
            (was it in love he fell?
            or in lust?
            oh, for princes, I fear, they are
            one and the same.)
And finally, as the meal came to a close,
the prince asked what the thief had stolen.

A week later, the prince's betrothal was announced.
How did he convince his father? His mother?
All the nobles whose daughters could now not be queen?
Was it the woman's demand, or the prince's?
Oh, that is a question with an answer no one knows.
The woman smiled, or so was reported,
whenever she was seen in public.

Never once, though, it is recorded
did our future queen visit the palace by the shore.

Our king died not long after his son wed
the dark-eyed, dark-haired woman
whose history no one knew.
Stories were told, questions were asked,
but it was said how the prince loved her so
and so it was done.
But our king died and
our kind-hearted prince ascended.

Our queen was gracious, our queen was kind,
our queen walked among the commoners with ease;
but never, it seemed, did she spend time with the nobility.
She would sit quietly beside our king during judgements, smiling.
She would speak with minstrels, with artisans—
she commissioned portraits of the ocean,
had minstrels sing all the songs of the sea they knew.
Why, then, did she never visit the palace by the shore?

They had a daughter, then a son.
The kingdom rejoiced.
The queen smiled as the light in her eyes dimmed.

He was a good man, our king.
                    So the stories tell.

Our tale closes with this:
          there was a fire.
Both the prince and princess were saved.
Our king was found,
but 'twas not the fire that killed him.
And our queen?
Our well-spoken and straight-spined queen?
          She vanished.

However, whenever the prince and princess
          (who were raised by their grandmother,
          who became regent for the prince)
spent time at the palace at the shore

and went walking along the water,
so it is said,
a woman would come from the sea,
would walk with them and sing,
and kiss them goodbye before sinking back into the waves.

Reflection

She wakes once a year, alone,
        (as she is every year)
and wanders the castle, seeking any change.
             Every year,
               there is no change.

As the sun sets, every year,
        she steps in front of the mirror

        to murmur, *Mirror mirror.*

(the first time, her voice was forceful, a command—
        but every year, her strength is less.)

        Who of the fairest remains?

The mirror answers the same, year after year after year.

        My princess, in your sleep,
        you are the fairest, 'tis true.
        But there is a merchant's daughter,
        soon to blossom into womanhood,
        *and they call her **Beauty**—*
    She, my princess, soon shall grow fairer than you.

She returns to her tower, trudging past the skeletons,
        (guards, servants, courtiers, family)
looks out the window to catch the last of the light,

        and then falls back into her bed.

Crucify Me

Silver
litters the floor, stirs up
dust. Above, the sun baths
the sky pale gold. Light
hits the coins, glinting with
shameful glee. He cannot look
away, staring into the sun,
wondering where he went wrong.

Silver
fills his sight, all he
sees and all he knows.

Silver
cold in his grip, clenched
tight in a traitor's fist.
With a curse he throws
it all at the grinning
jesters who think they've won.

Silver
streaks across the sky. Coarse
rope against his skin, tight
around his throat. The clouds
above are calm and knowing;
he wonders where he went
wrong, and then with a
twist, he wonders no more.

>   *Crucify me, Father.*
>   *Crucify me for my sins.*
>   *I languish, silver clenched in my fist.*
>   *Crucify me, Father.*
>   *Do you not hear me repent?*

Sea Witch

In the
deep
dark
where no light has ever shone

there *s h e* rests

on a throne of tattered bone
remnants of beasts long gone

And *s h e* laughs

causing whirlpools
causing hurricanes
for the King of the Sea
(arrogant, contemptuous
traitorous, foul)
rages in his grief, sinking more ships
in a single day

than *s h e* ever has

What better vengeance could there be?

For
so
long

s h e

has waited and now
at
last—

Anger has ever caused
the King of the Sea to falter
and the death of his beloved child
—for a *human*—
Oh, it's so delicious, delightful

for is he furious or mournful?
Both at once,
deliciously
delightfully
furiously mournful

And the sea
swallows cities,
swamps continents
consumes all to the bone

and   *s h e*   laughs

in the
deep
dark
and then

s h e

rises
for the time has come at last
the time   *s h e*   has
hungered for
the time   *s h e*   has
languished for

The beasts from the
deep
dark
follow

as
s h e

rises
from
the
depths

i n s a t i a b l e

Toll

The bridge crosses the river—
        Wide,
             deep.
Frequent drownings:
     Attempts to ford.

Bones dot the riverbed,
        scored by sharp bitemark scars.

The price to safely cross:
           Brave the troll's hunger.
He built the strongest bridge
     and the cost is consumption.

Mary, Mother of God

i wonder how you,
      Mary, Mother of God,
felt when the
      Spirit
tore through you, not even
seeking permission, invading you
in the rape of rapes—
did you feel anger, for even
a moment, or merely pain? the
      Child
you bore was the most important in
the world: did you ever feel
favored that you, of all women,
were chosen to bear the
      King?

      Joseph
believed he was chosen,
      Son of David,
that
      God
honored him with the care of the
      King.
      dear Mary,
we know the truth—it was you picked,
you the herald and bearer.
you were the choice out of all creation;
you were picked,
      dearest of Marys:
you were the
      Mother of God.

are you not proud, little maid of Nazareth?
ah, but pride is a sin—were you excited
to be the one who bore the
      King?
you were the greatest woman in the world,
      Mary, Mother of God—

you were
>> the Holy Raped.

>> Mary,
did you ever dare to question
>> Him
for taking you?
did you ever scream and cry,
beg the sky *why* and fall to your knees?
did you demand, with broken innocence
and righteous fury, why
>> He
shattered through you,
breaking and mending you, leaving a child?
did you once feel terrified?

after you laid eyes on your
>> Child,
did your soul heal? was all forgiven?
did you fall in love?
when you kissed the
>> King,
did you wonder *why me?*

i'm sure you never asked
>> Joseph—
just a man, what could he know?
and you couldn't ask your mother—
she'd never understand; how could she?
she never felt
>> God's hand
rip through her, leaving such a seed,
a spark of life and revolution,
the salvation of humanity.

tell me,
>> dear Mary,
if you can hear me from paradise
—as the
>> Mother of God,
I'm sure you made it there—did you ever

demand an explanation of your
        Child's Father?
did you once ask why? or did you merely
bow your head and keep on your way,
like a good daughter of your time?
was it love,
        Mary?
or duty? or, for you,
were they the same?

Sea Salt

Warmth comes with the light,
    drying the salt from her skin
        until the sea is only in her
            sweat and tears.
With her steps on the harsh ground,
    so little soft on land,
        things are hard and cold—
           save the fire and the sun
             and the cloth her prince's
          servants drape on her.
Baths hurt, being so close yet so far from home,
    and dusk brings warnings from the witch:
        time passing but no yes, no kiss, no marriage.
Why is she here,
    a daughter of the sea on dirt?
Storms harass the coast, her family's lament,
    and she stands on trembling legs,
        singing the waters to calm.
Her sisters know the ending looms
    and yet no kiss,
        an ocean in her sweat and her tears
          as the prince she loves weds another.
He doesn't know because the sea's daughter cannot speak
    and the blade is cold in her hands,
        her sisters' song loud in her heart,
          her survival dependent on his demise.
The moon is her mother and the hurricane her father,
    and no, she will not hurt the man she loves.
She leaves, knife falling from shaking fingers,
    and the water embraces her for a single moment,
        and her sisters scream,
        and her mother weeps,
        and her father rages,
    but the prince doesn't know
        and the young woman who loved him,
          who smiled so beautifully and laughed so silently,
          who looked at everything with wonder,
            who watched him with adoring eyes—
        she is gone forever to pay the witch,

her life for her love,
forever in the ocean now,
ever part of the waves as sea foam.

Diamonds and Blood

The mirror shatters.

She grins, twirling around the floor,
the prince's eyes only on her,
music spiraling, whispers on the air.
She smiles, stepping in,
his hands firm on her hips.

Godmother's magic gleams,
diamonds and pearls sparkling,
silver tiara on dark hair,
her lips blood red.
The prince does not look away.

The clock strikes a quarter 'til;
she takes no notice.
The spell will not fade,
still draining her silly sister's life.
            Beware, my dear, Godmother murmured,
but she was well prepared.

There is a price to magic,
always, no matter what fools say.
There is a price that must be paid.
She leans into the prince,
presses her lips to his throat,
inhales his scent.

The clock strikes midnight.
In a house on the edge of town,
a girl gasps her last breath,
pooled blood drying on the floor.

            Beware, my dear, Godmother murmured,
but she smiled, blade in hand,
and her silly sister waited too long to flinch.
The prince lowers his head,
captivated by her gaze,

her tanned arms, gloved hands,
the glinting jewels on her chest.

They ask:
> *Who is she?*
> *Where has she been?*
> *She's so beautiful.*
> *I haven't a chance with the prince.*

She laughs, pressing against him,
a murmur rising on the breeze
no one else hears.
A quarter after, half past,
and then one is gone.

A domineering mother discovers her daughter's corpse
in a house on the edge of town.
No servants remain employed here,
only a dead husband's child
who silently obeyed as all her rights were stripped away.

Beware, my dear, Godmother warned
but she did nothing as the girl
twisted the magic to her will.

Marry me, the prince begs
as they walk in the garden,
hand clutching hers so tightly both ache.
Become my wife, please, he begs,
kissing her breathless,
the scent of roses rising on the air.

Yes, she whispers
and the first enchantment breaks.

Beware my dear, Godmother sighs.

The sun rises
and another woman dies
in a house on the edge of town.

The prince is caught,
gazing at her in rags,
dark hair loose over her shoulders,
all jewels gone.
He takes her hand,
presses her knuckles to his lips.

She never returns to
the house on the edge of town.
No one sets foot in the house:
the earth swallows it—
A high cost indeed,
but she is clever enough to not pay.

       Beware my dear, Godmother whispers
as she kisses the prince,
a tiara glinting on her head.
She is wed to a prince
and soon
—sooner than anyone expects—
she will be queen.
       Beware my dear, Godmother warns,
but no one hears.

Godmother once promised to protect a child.
She soon wished she hadn't
but magic is tricky and exacting,
and she is bound tight.
A merchant's daughter becomes a slave,
and a slave becomes a queen.

The mirror shatters.
       Beware, my dear, the queen tells her daughter,
magic singeing the air
as glass pieces back together,
the princess gasping in awe.
       Learn, my sweet, the queen laughs,
and Godmother, far away, closes her eyes.

Storybook Histories

Snow White

No red apples grow in the castle orchard.
No one sells red apples in the markets.
She craves apple pie but cannot bear the taste.

The Princess and the Pea

The queen mother insists on
peas with every meal,
breakfast to dinner to midnight snacks.

The queen has never
enjoyed peas.

The Little Mermaid

She drops back home, into the shallows,
           and lets the water pull her away from
      the prince's marriage bed, and she stares
  at the sky as she falls
                      away into the waves.

The Sleeping Beauty in the Wood

nicks in the shining blade
scars scored from stone thorns
metal shrieks and finally shatters
blood dots along through dirt
another life lost in dust

Cindermaid

Her ladies coo over her
roughened hands
and her
scarred knees.

Tonics and powders and nightly soaks
soften her skin
but her back still aches.

Rumpelstiltskin

The straw is
rough
against her skin,
scrapes dotted with blood.

The gold,
though gleaming,
leaves her cold.

Hansel and Gretel

She dismembers the boy
before skinning the meat;
separates the pieces—
   some to boil,
   some to bake,
   some to store for the lean months.

The girl sobs herself unconscious
while the meat cooks.

The Frog Prince

The little golden ball
slips from her fingers,
a single
      plop
into the bottom of the well

She reaches, almost
falls, grasping; the edge
                    digs into her palms

Behind her, a
      croak

The Goose Girl

Such fine cloth against her
skin, soft, sweet—
Years, she's dreamt of this.

The princess weeps;
the no-longer-servant ignores the tears,
taking her place
beneath the tiara,
in the soon-to-be wedding bed.

Hoofbeats   on   in   dreams.
        ring   stone   her

The Seventh Mrs. de Winter

Do not enter this room, though it is locked
and I have all the keys on this ring,
and though this entire house
is to call me *Mistress* now.
He left me here to wait while he travels,
and the house in its entirety is mine.
       I have the key.
Why forbid my entrance
                   to this one room?

          (Ghosts linger here,
          crying at night, crying through the day,
          weeping everywhere for me to
          Leave this place.
          Sister, run before it's too late.)

The key,
the smallest key,
the golden key:
       in my dreams,
              I watch it bleed.
Blood drips,
       drop
             by
                 drop,
                     p o o l s
at my feet.
Footprints follow me,
              but not where I stepped.
Footprints follow me
and I
wake,
       a scream caught in my throat,
       the key in my hand.

This one room
I am to never enter.
This one room
       beyond my sight,

beyond my reach,
beyond the proclamation
that
    I
      am
         Mistress
of this domain.
A single room in a castle of rooms.
What
    hides,
    lurks,
    waits inside?

      (Ghosts linger here,
      calling my name, calling me sister, pleading,
      Leave. Run before it's too late.)

Golden key clutched by aching fingers, I
    stride down the hall to the single room I
    have never seen, the single room
the master of this house ordered I
    never enter or even approach.

      The key slides easily into the lock. I do not
      even turn the knob. The door opens. I step
      into the room, close my eyes. I breathe in
      the stench of dried blood.
         Sister, the ghosts sigh.

I pull the door shut behind me
and return to my own room,
where the servants draw me a bath.
I soak until the water cools.

Blood drips from the key.
My husband should arrive tomorrow;
wedded for a month and only a week
spent in each other's company,
in learning to be man and wife.
      I am not the first—

I counted the skulls,
placed on the walls
like hunting trophies:
      six of them,   six women before me,
      six wives ordered to never
open the door,   six who disobeyed.

I walk through my domain
as the servants clean it top to bottom,
           all except that one room.
The stench of dried blood follows me.
Horseshoes on cobblestone tell me
the master of the house has come home.

The golden key in hand,
     I wait.
Sister, the ghosts sigh.
           I am not the first wife.

Sisters, I vow, setting the key on his bed.
       My sisters, I shall be the last.

let this cup pass from Me

Mother, forgive me, says the Son,
hanging limp on a Cross.

Oh, my Son, my Son, the Mother cries,
has been crying, will always cry.

No Mother can know what will
become

of her Child—
No Mother is ever

given a
choice.

Selkie Wife

He found the skin one beautiful day, midmorning and bright.
He kept it, of course, hidden well out of sight.
She searched and searched and finally knocked on the door.
He knew her for what she was and told her,
"Be my wife." She agreed, of course. Don't they always?

> *Yes*
> *they do*
> *at first*

He had work that took him far from home, but
now he had a wife to clean and have dinner
ready when he came tromping in. He claimed her at
night, this lovely woman who could not say no or
risk her true-self destroyed. She bore him two fine sons
and a pretty daughter and she smiled and kissed him,
always listening for the sea whenever he was inside her.

> *The sea*
> *the sea*
> *the sea*
> *roaring in wait*

He never went to the skin. Truthfully, he forgot where
he'd hidden it, far from prying eyes, far from the
sea as their village could be. His sons grew tall
and worked beside him, out on the ocean where seals
played. His daughter heard the sea no matter where in
town she went, and one day, in a hole in
the ground in a box of stone and shell she
found a luxurious fur. Never had she seen something so
lovely. Of course, she brought it home to her mama.

> *Home again*
> *my love*
> *home again*
> *soon*

One touch and she knew. One glance and she yearned.
She smelled the salt air, heard the wind churning up
the water, and she told her daughter, "Don't tell your
father." Ocean howled in the words as her daughter swore.

> *Years taken*
> *will be*
> *taken back*

She waited until the children were in bed, until her
husband snored, barely able to use her before falling asleep,
until the moon was high, high as the sun the
day she'd been stolen. She waited until she could wait
no moment longer. She woke him with a kiss and
he turned to her sleepily, stretching out his neck as
he sought another. Never had she been stronger as when
she kissed his throat with the blade used for slicing
fruit. He choked, gurgled, reached for her with fumbling hands
and she watched, calm as the shallows, as he collapsed.

> *They always stay*
> *until they don't*

Their sons slept on but their daughter met her at
the door. "Will you come with me?" she asked, home
warm in her hands. "I'll come with you to the
shore," her daughter said, crashing waves loud in her ears.

> *Home again*
> *home again*
> *home again*
> *soon*

She tore off a woman's nightclothes; she kicked away a woman's
shoes. Her daughter watched and stayed silent until they both stood
in the sea, her skin around her shoulders about to make
her whole again. "Wait," said her daughter, reaching for her. "I've
heard the sea all my life, too." She looked her daughter
in the eye as the girl asked, "Am I like you?"

Freed
    freedom
        free
           warm waters
           cold waters
   coming to me

"You could be," she answered. Her daughter glanced back
to the town, to the moon high above the
water, to her mother, wild as the wind. Her
brothers slept; she knew her father was dead. Waves
crashed on the shore and a storm built on
the air. Her mother held out a hand and
her daughter closed her eyes and together they dove
beneath the water both as they should be again.

     Swim far
     from the shore
     you've walked
     the shore you
     were taken from

There was no husband in the sea; she had yet been
too young, still curious and naïve about landfolk. There was no
family in the sea; they had all moved on when she
didn't come home. But she had her daughter, and her freedom,
and the entire sea. "Are you happy?" her daughter asked, looping
and diving and laughing. "Yes," she laughed in reply. "Oh, yes."

    Don't leave your skin on land
        we caution our daughters
    Don't trust in landfolk
        we warn our sons
    No one will fight for you
        we tell our children
    You must fight for yourself

She watched her daughter chasing fish and investigating whales, and
she knew, deep down where still-warm blood pooled across
the bed, that her daughter would always be safe, always
be free, no matter the blood spilt upon the ground.

Fare(well)

The manor is quiet now;
we're frightened to break the
silence, to draw Mother's attention—
She has raged every day
since you left in magic
and pearls, in a gown
of stars in a midnight
sky.
      We never understood everything
you did for us; now
we must do it ourselves.
You smiled even when your
fingers must have burned, when
standing still itself sent aches
through your bones. You are
gone.
      I never imagined this
manor without your swift steps,
your soft voice, your hands
brushing our hair. You are
gone, sister, in a palace
with servants of your own—
You surely treat them better
than we ever treated you.

Mother of Knowledge

Ah, my father (lover), I did
ask forgiveness of you and our Maker,
the King of the Garden who formed us both.
I came of you, son of dust (Yahweh).
I came of you and you fell.
                              In love? Yes.
Yahweh formed me
                    for you.
          Am I
mother of man,
granddaughter of dust?
          I am nothing but
          yours.

I gave you
a gift
from the serpent.
I sought to please you—
But before you took that mouthful,
lover dear, I was more.
                    More than you,
I came of you, but I knew first.
                    Before you took that mouthful
                              —my gift—
          I was more.

I came of (for) you—
          a toy, a companion, a mate.
Every being had another
of their own—and there you
were, dear lover, alone but
for our Creator, our Lord.
You had Him first,
          were created first,
born of love and will and dust.
          I came of you.

He, our King (of the Garden), gave us the world
with but one rule:
        a single tree He left beyond our touch.

I did not intend to disobey Him; like you,
I had no idea what disobedience was.
But that serpent—
such a sensuous, beautiful creature—
told me if I ate of the (forbidden) tree
        I could learn.
I listened to the serpent—
listening is no sin.
But then I plucked the fruit,
my love(r), and I took a lingering bite.

At first I tasted dust (like you).
But then the juices filled my mouth
and flowed down my throat—
so exquisite, it tasted of Heaven.
                (what I imagined
                of Heaven's taste)

I wanted more, to eat it all,
and sometimes, I wish I had.
But instead I brought it to you,
my father, and offered you a taste.

You put your lips to the fruit,
licked it—you
feared,   *(how did*
     darling,   *that first*
though I   *taste of*
     never did.   *fear feel?)*

Knowledge flowed through me—
like the serpent said, I had
        become
           a god.

Is godhood a crime?
I have asked forgiveness
of you and the Maker,
but I—oh, father (lover),
never once did I mean it.

                    (am i

                         mother
                    of the first
                         lie?)

I came of (for) you.
But I learned before you.
          I came of you and you fell.
You know pain and fear because of me.
But think of this—
would joy or love exist without them?
In the garden we had no emotion,
but here in the wide, cold world—
I *feel*, lover (father).

          And I do not regret it.

Shards

"What did she see, when she looked into you?"
the soon-to-be-queen asks the mirror,
dark hair braided and swinging behind her
as she paces in front of the glass.

The mirror does not answer.

"What did she see, when she looked into you?"
the queen asks the mirror,
dark hair falling in waves down her back,
golden crown glinting in candlelight.

The mirror does not answer.

"Why does she spend hours gazing into you?"
the princess asks the mirror,
her hair a burnished bronze like her father's,
her skin as ruddy as his, despite her mother's sighs.

The mirror answers:
> *Oh, sweet girl, you'll learn in time.*

Twisted Tales

I.

"Girl! Up! Where's our breakfast?"
   hearth long grown cold
   glittering glass in growing light
"Girl! Answer me! Where are you?"
   ash-stained skin
   calloused fingers to never move again

II.

Glimmering glass in midmorning light
Red rose lips, bloodless skin
Dying grass and still-stale air
Pale flakes melting as they fall
    Princess mourned
    Queen triumphant

III.

    The skulls grin
  Twining   vines   vines twining
      Bloodstained   thorns
Swords swallowed in undergrowth
     Hands broken and rotten
   The beauty sleeps

IV.

forest floor—pale and soft
   fallen from on high
     in desperate flight

crimson drying on white
   call silenced mid-cry
     never again to rise—

V.

tower
   collapsed,   magic   stolen, gone,
            lost when laughter fled
stone crumbled   on
       dead grass, golden hair

on freezing wind   blown away

VI.

Bitingly bitter breeze;
     icy hair tugged by freezing water.
  "My sister dear," calls a voice,
          tone a loving lie.
  "My dear sister," calls a voice.
The bitingly bitter breeze blows.

VII.

The moon shines on the stones,
     little feet pattering along an untrod path,
         brother and sister in the woods seeking home.

"Delicious!" the witch declares, turning
     to hold the spoon to the girl's mouth.
         "Taste your brother, dear."

exeunt

And Into The Sky

Princesses sit in towers, forgotten
Princes ride their noble steeds into the sunset, unforgiven
And the witches all cackle 'round the pots and stir the brew

One by one, two by two,
'round the roses red we go

Dragons spurt their fire up into the blood-drenched clouds
Unicorns gallop into the sea
Wolves howl in the night to the moon, begging

And no one hears, no one ever hears

Three by three, four by four,
'round the roses red we go

Spread your wings, the minstrels chant
Spread your wings and soar away
Spread your wings, dearest one—you, at least, can escape

The tiara balances on a precipice
The scepter shatters on the stones
The throne rusts, covered by dust

And no one cares, no one ever cares

Scheherazade's voice fails and the king takes her life
Icarus' wings don't melt and he soars into the sun
Cinderella lives happily ever after, but Snow White dies—

Isn't life a grand fairytale?

Five by five, six by six
'round the roses red we go

The princesses fade into the shadows
The princes burn come light of day
And no one ever thought it would end

III

No one ever thought it could end
Legends never die

Legends aren't supposed to die

Seven by seven, eight by eight
'round the roses red we go

Mary, Mary, quite contrary
Didn't you wed Little Boy Blue?

Where is Valiant, and Charming?
Where are the heroes to slay the dragons—
Why has Heracles gone away?

Medusa wasn't supposed to kill Perseus—
Get your legends straight

Nine by nine, ten by ten
'round the roses red we go

Can't we start again?
I don't think I like where this is going...

Who's that on the pale horse?
And what follows behind him?

Give to me the sky

End Notes

The Horse Fair—painted by Rosa Bonheur between 1852 and 1855; currently at the Metropolitan Museum of Art in New York, New York.

Resurrected Trees—full quote: "I am born a poet... that is my nature and vocation" (p. xiv) from Yoder, R.A. (1978). *Emerson and the Orphic poet in America.* Berkley, California: University of California Press.

The Seventh Mrs. de Winter—title references *Rebecca* by Daphne de Maurier.

let this cup pass from Me—biblical reference, Matthew 26:39.

ABOUT ATMOSPHERE PRESS

Atmosphere Press is an independent, full-service publisher for excellent books in all genres and for all audiences. Learn more about what we do at atmospherepress.com.

We encourage you to check out some of Atmosphere's latest releases, which are available at Amazon.com and via order from your local bookstore:

The Distance from Odessa, poetry by Carol Seitchik

How It Shone, poetry by Katherine Barham

Wind Bells, poetry in English and Tagalog by Jessica Perez Dimalibot

Meraki, poetry by Tobi-Hope Jieun Park

Impression, poetry by Charnjit Gill

Aching to be Human, poetry by Stormy Abel

Love is Blood, Love is Fabric, poetry by Mary De La Fuente

How to Hypnotize a Lobster, poetry by Kristin Rose Jutras

The Mercer Stands Burning, night poems by John Pietaro

Calls for Help, poetry by Greg T. Miraglia

Lost in the Greenwood, poetry by Ellen Roberts Young

Blessed Arrangement, poetry by Larry Levy

Lovely Dregs, poetry by Richard Sipe

Out of the Dark, poetry by William Guest

Shadow Truths, poetry by V. Rendina

A Synonym for Home, poetry by Kimberly Jarchow

The Cry of Being Born, poetry by Carol Mariano

Big Man Small Europe, poetry by Tristan Niskanen

Lucid_Malware.zip, poetry by Dylan Sonderman

The Unordering of Days, poetry by Jessica Palmer

It's Not About You, poetry by Daniel Casey

A Dream of Wide Water, poetry by Sharon Whitehill

Radical Dances of the Ferocious Kind, poetry by Tina Tru

ABOUT THE AUTHOR

Born and raised in Baton Rouge, Louisiana, Laura Williams cannot remember a time she did not love to read; her passion for writing came later, but poetry has been her life-long love. The younger middle child of four, she has been blessed with a large, close-knit family. She is in the process of earning her doctorate in education, focusing on adult literacy, at Louisiana State University and lives with two mischievous cats.

CPSIA information can be obtained
at www.ICGtesting.com
Printed in the USA
LVHW090516170721
692931LV00007B/920